YoungWriters

The Big Green Poetry Machine

Yorkshire

Edited by Annabel Cook

YoungWriters
First published in Great Britain in 2008 by:
Young Writers
Remus House
Coltsfoot Drive
Peterborough
PE2 9JX
Telephone: 01733 890066
Website: www.youngwriters.co.uk

SB ISBN 978-1 84431 733 2

Foreword

Young Writers' Big Green Poetry Machine is a showcase for our nation's most brilliant young poets to share their thoughts, hopes and fears for the planet they call home.

Young Writers was established in 1991 to nurture creativity in our children and young adults, to give them an interest in poetry and an outlet to express themselves. Seeing their work in print will encourage them to keep writing as they grow, and become our poets of tomorrow.

Selecting the poems has been challenging and immensely rewarding. The effort and imagination invested by these young writers makes their poems a pleasure to enjoy reading time and time again.

Contents

The Poems

Don't Let Animals Die

D on't make it happen
O rang-utans need your help so help them
N ever let them down
T ell them how much you care about them

L et the world know about them
E nough is enough, help them
T he pandas need your help

T he animals need your help
H ear them cry for your help
E very animals needs your help

A nything can happen
N ever forget this poem
I t will never happen if we don't work together
M any lives need your help
A lways keep this in your mind
L et us all be kind
S o let yourself shine

D on't forget there is always help
I want to help them, do you?
E ven this is up to you.

Bethany Druett (10)
Acomb Primary School, York

Animal Extinction

Endangered animals are amazing,
Hunted for features because they are beautiful creatures.
Bones are crushed into powder,
Fur from big cats.
Hunters kill them, although the animals are dangerous,
No one should hurt them, it just is not right
Animals become extinct,
No one has a reason,
All because they're big and lovely creatures.

Hannah Barnett (9)
Acomb Primary School, York

Recycling

Recycling bottles in one box, in another, tins
So put your recycling into the bin
And watch it get thrown into the van
Recycling is good
Recycling is good for the environment
So don't throw your cans onto the floor, put them into the bin
Paper on the floor, pick it up and put it into the bin.

Jack Franks (9)
Acomb Primary School, York

Extinct

A nimals in danger.
N ow most of them are extinct.
I n Africa sadly seven species are gone.
M e and you could save the world.
A nimals need the love and care.
L ook what your donations can do.
S ave the animals!

Paige Jones (10)
Acomb Primary School, York

Wicked War

W icked war, exciting war, dangerous war.
A mazing war, destructive, colourful, but vile.
R ushing war, rickety, rock on the spot.
Just try to do something about this pollution.
Quick or else you'll regret it!

Aaron Gilroy (9)
Acomb Primary School, York

Save The Animals

S ave the animals from danger.
A little donation might help.
V iolence is not the right thing for animals.
E ven though they need help.

T hey are in terrible danger.
H elp them now, quickly, before they die.
E ven though they are in attack.

A nimals are dying so get help.
N ever let down an animal who needs help.
I n the Earth animals need food and water.
M ost animals live, just like you and me.
A ll of the animals are destroyed.
L iving in this world is hard.
S ave the animals, live in this same world.
We just have to get along.

Sheela Gopalaswamy
Acomb Primary School, York

Recycle Today

R ecycle your rubbish
E nd the landfill
C ome and get your recycle bin
Y ou need to help the environment
C ome and make the world a different place
L ove the Earth
E nd the evilness of the rubbish

T oday could be a big difference
O ne thing will change everything
D on't give up
A nything you want to recycle come now
Y ou know you want to save the world.

Chelsea Wyard (11)
Acomb Primary School, York

Loving Animals

A nimals could be saved, animals could be seen.
N aughty animals, good animals, natural animals.
I love animals.
M onkeys bouncing tree to tree.
A nimals need food, animals need water.
L ots of incredible animals.
S o many animals, birds and fishes.

Tanya Page (9)
Acomb Primary School, York

Endangered Animals!

There are lots of different animals right around the globe,
There's pandas, turtles, dolphins and other animals too.
They're very close to extinction that's what you need to know,
So you need to stop hunting and catching them as well.

A rhinoceros is a strong and powerful creature,
But people hunt them down for their very special feature.
You need to understand what it all means
And save the Earth and wildlife so the world it gleams.

Esther Raxworthy (10)
Acomb Primary School, York

Recycling

R ecycling is good for the environment
E co kids come and make an eco garden
C ome and recycle your peelings in the compost bin
Y ou just come and get your bin for free
C ome and recycle at your supermarkets for free
L ying on the sofa, come and recycle instead
I n the world people are homeless
N othing but bones
G ardens are good for playing in instead of on the consoles.

James Gallacher (10)
Acomb Primary School, York

Orang-Utans Are Cool!

I saw him one day in the zoo,
Oh! Believe me he stared at me too.
Just wonder what happens out there,
Just give some money and show that you care!
'To the treetops!' the tree cutters shout,
'Argh! Help us!' all the orang-utans cry out.
The zookeepers to the rescue! You know what happens!
Oh I do! The zookeepers take the orang-utans into a canoe!
So come on! Come and see them at the zoo!

Bethany Howse (10)
Acomb Primary School, York

Litter Destroys The Earth

L itter destroys the Earth
I f you see litter pick it up and put it in the bin
T each people not to litter
T he more you litter you'll get a fine
E vaporate litter
R ecycle the litter.

Calvin McShane (9)
Acomb Primary School, York

Recycling

R emember the 3 Rs - reduce, reuse and recycle
E verybody should do the deed
C an you take part in saving the environment?
Y our rubbish could turn into cool gifts!
C an't be very hard
L ove to recycle!
I f you recycle a glass bottle you will save enough energy to
power a computer for 25 minutes
N othing can go wrong if you recycle
G oing, going, *gone!*

Sarah Zbadynski (11)
Acomb Primary School, York

Global Warming

Change the world and help global warming,
Stop the cars and stop the polluting.

Alarming the Earth
And allowing global warming's birth.

International panic,
We need a life-saver, not a mechanic.

The world is getting warmer
And we're having a trauma.

The weather is changing,
Lives are changing.

Maisie Wilson (10)
Acomb Primary School, York

Stop!

A ll you have to do is stop hunting.
N ever give up, it is important.
I n the world there's loads of animals,
M any close to extinction.
A lways helping each other in each way,
L eopards leaping in the bushes to catch their prey,
S nakes sliding in the jungle, slithering around,
so stop hunting right now!

Jacob Schofield (10)
Acomb Primary School, York

Homeless

H omelessness is hard to help
O h those poor people have to yelp
M y grandad is homeless
E ncased in a world of badness
L iving on your own makes you really mad
E verything is really, really bad
S ome people see me every day
S ome time later they go away.

Lewis Seton (10)
Acomb Primary School, York

The Wrong Bin

Hello,
Down here right on the floor,
People don't care anymore.
Once we are used we're no use to them,
So then it happens all over again.
Throw us away and fill us with sin,
But even when they do it, they get the wrong bin.
Black is for darkness,
Blue is for good,
Green is for things like cardboard and wood!
So please pick me up, oh thank you
And in the green one, yes that's right,
You picked the right bin.

Callum Coultish (9)
Camblesforth Community Primary School, Selby

Animals In Danger

Animals in danger
Please call the rangers
Some of them surviving
The other ones are dying
Please call the rangers
Animals in danger
The big word extinction
Is all about the distinction
Animals in danger
Please call the rangers
Red ones, blue ones
Different coloured cool ones
Please save the animals
And the big old mammals
Some big, some small, some so tall
Because . . .
Animals in danger
Please call the rangers.

Bethany Kerrigan (10)
Camblesforth Community Primary School, Selby

The Life Cycle Of Paper

I was once inside a tree with all of my good friends
And then one day I hurt my head
And the tree came tumbling down, down, down
The tree came tumbling down
We were then taken to a workshop and turned into paper
We were taken to a shop and were sold next day
And were used when they got home, home, home
I was used when they got home
So I recommend recycling all of your paper
We will get used again and again
And don't waste paper, recycle today.

Declan Purvis (10)
Camblesforth Community Primary School, Selby

Don't Kill The Animals

The rainforest is great, the rainforest is green
You're killing the animals' homes
Look what you're doing to the world
Look what you're doing to the animals
If you keep doing it sooner or later they will become extinct
And then the world will be a horrible place.

Ryan James Donald Brind (9)
Camblesforth Community Primary School, Selby

Animals In Danger, Help!

Poor animals in danger
We don't even care
Why don't we start thinking about it now
Some animals live, some die, some suffer, some survive
Why are we killing? How do they deserve it?
So why are we doing it to them?
Stop now, stop now, stop now, stop now!
Why are we doing it?

Abigail Singleton (9)
Camblesforth Community Primary School, Selby

Recycling King

Recycle, recycle, do bin, do win
Just recycle, recycle, recycle

Recycle, recycle, the things you don't need
Then you will take the lead

Recycle and save the world
Then you will say the word

Recycle, recycle the things you don't need
Then you will take the lead.

Luke Robert Russell (10)
Camblesforth Community Primary School, Selby

Recycle And Live

Recycle, recycle,
Don't bin,
Don't waste,
Just recycle it.
Recycle glass bottles
And plastic bottles and things, recycle!
Recycle things which are reusable,
Recycle things that people need.

Recycle, recycle, don't bin,
You'll win.

Carl Clarke (9)
Camblesforth Community Primary School, Selby

Why Does It Matter?

Why does it matter what skin colour you are?
Does that change what your personalities are?
Do I care if you have black or white skin,
From Africa or Egypt, from China or Berlin?
Do you think you're big and tough?
You bully people but you're the real wuss.

Gemma Huddlestone (10)
Camblesforth Community Primary School, Selby

Global Warming

Put the litter away, it will slowly fade away
Recycle every day, it's cruel to the world today
All the plastic and tin doesn't belong on the floor
It belongs in the bin
The card and the paper could be used again and again
If you litter don't speed away
You could get caught one of these days
Recycling is good, do it today!

Megan Kimberly Mitchell (10)
Camblesforth Community Primary School, Selby

Litterbugs!

If you've got litter don't throw it away,
Chuck it in a recycle bin so it will fade away.
Put your litter in the green bin,
No more litter bugs.
People gossip about global warming,
But they don't do anything about it.
Governors can you listen, we need to do something now!
You're hurting the animals, don't throw rubbish away.
Make a collage with your litter,
Act now people!

Laura Jane Croft (10)
Camblesforth Community Primary School, Selby

A New Start

If you're chucking paper
If you're chucking card
Don't use the floor as a bin
It could be a new start
Since this is the world we'll grow up in
Let's use the recycle bins.

Erin Harpham (10)
Camblesforth Community Primary School, Selby

If You Recycle

If you recycle everything will live
Blue is for glass, green is for cars
If you recycle lifecycles will continue
If you recycle listen to me
If you recycle creatures will live
So recycle, don't bin, *recycle.*

Jonathan Croft (10)
Camblesforth Community Primary School, Selby

No More Animals

Animals, animals, animals everywhere,
They are so kind to you and yet you don't even care.
If you look in the future, look for animals in the night,
But when you've looked everywhere, your face will go bright white.
There are no animals anywhere, because you've killed them all,
And there isn't any more, they're at the other side of the wall.
You can't carry on like this, you have to stop now,
If you stop this instant, there will not be any wall.

Holly Guilar (10)
Camblesforth Community Primary School, Selby

Recycling

You need to recycle, 1, 2, 3
Choose the right bin
Or your life will be grim
The green one's for paper
The blue one's for glass
The floor is no place for all this trash
Lots of lovely trees, chop, chop, chop
Homes are destroyed and paper is cut
Recycle, recycle, *recycle.*

Olivia Murphy (10)
Camblesforth Community Primary School, Selby

Recycling

Take your trash to your recycling centre,
There's ones for plastic, paper, glass,
Wood, fabric, tins, cans and tyres,
So don't bin it!
Recycle it!
Recycle for the world's sake.

Hayden Steven Clark (10)
Camblesforth Community Primary School, Selby

Cruel Not Cool

Some people think it's cool,
But I think it's cruel.
Mother Nature will get you later
For the things you have done,
So don't use a gun.
No one will win,
But you might break your shin.
So listen to this before you bomb again,
Don't be insane, use your brain.
Things will never be the same.
So don't be lame, please be nice,
Be nice and eat rice
And think twice before you kill again.

Benjamin William Morris (10)
Camblesforth Community Primary School, Selby

Bad Not Good

Save the meat
Save the life of a kind
If we don't extinction will come
And the kind will be gone, gone, gone
Save the pig
Save the lamb
Save the chicken
Save, save, save them
If we don't they will be gone
So stop it now or else
So recycle.

Harry Kent (10)
Camblesforth Community Primary School, Selby

Emperor Of Litter

If you're good or you're bad,
If you're happy or sad,
Everyone does it the same.
You drop it down, it comes up again,
So you drop it down again and again.
Litter is bad, litter is cruel,
You don't need to cry, you don't need to say,
All you need to do is act today.
Put it in a bin, don't be a sin,
Put it away some day, put it away today.
Recycle for yourselves.

Katy Sarah Croft (10)
Camblesforth Community Primary School, Selby

Saving

Switch off lights before you go,
Keep your bin waste very low,
Recycle it bit by bit,
If we don't do all this,
Nature we're going to miss,
Don't keep our air polluted,
Keep it pure,
Because we just cannot endure,
Don't use chemicals to kill the weeds,
Just pull them out and plant the seeds,
Better environment we want to see,
A better world from creature to tree,
Save the world.

Katherine Dinsdale (7)
Coppice Valley Community Primary School, Harrogate

Recycle Rap

Helping the environment helps you
And your children's children too!
In the ground your rubbish goes
Which does not help the world's flow.
The rainforests are being cut down,
Which makes the whole word frown!
Filling the air with greenhouse gases,
Produces pollution in masses.
The 3Rs you can use are recycle, reduce and reuse,
Glass, clothes, tin and cans,
Can save the world hand in hand.
Diseases are spreading because of pollution
And if we die there will be no evolution!
This big green poem is about recycling,
So help by reusing, reducing and recycling!

Jasmine Romilly (10)
Coppice Valley Community Primary School, Harrogate

Recycling - It's Up To You

How can recycling help you?
Not to throw rubbish in the deep blue,
Polluting the air with greenhouse gases
And you can recycle lots of glasses.
Newspaper, clothes and lots more
Is a good way to help sure,
So help the world be a better place,
When you meet *rubbish* face to face.

Kirsty Walton (10)
Coppice Valley Community Primary School, Harrogate

The Invisible War

War is coming with the environment's anger
This has been caused by our carelessness
If we don't stop now we could be responsible
For such crimes as genocide and extinction

If we do stop now we can restart our world
And make it more environmentally friendly
With more nature parks and wildlife
And less human occupation space.

Joel Thornton (11)
Coppice Valley Community Primary School, Harrogate

Global Warming

Ice caps are melting
Antarctic animals are becoming extinct
Our home disappears
Recycle and reuse
Help us by bringing down fuel emissions
And bring us back to normal
The temperature is rising!
Animal population is falling
Think about the Earth.

Douglas Law (11)
Dishforth Airfield CP School, Thirsk

Untitled

Save the animals by
stopping deforestation.
Start recycling paper,
compost and old pieces of fruit.

Charlotte Pointon (10)
Dishforth Airfield CP School, Thirsk

Untitled

Stop! Save our world,
Recycle cans,
Stop littering, it is bad.
Save the trees and stop the madness,
Turn off lights and save energy,
Stop the pollution.

Nick Patterson (11)
Dishforth Airfield CP School, Thirsk

Trees

T ry and help us save the trees.
R ecycle and put paper in the green box please.
E very day we're using more and more.
E very day birds are getting sore.
S ave our souls!

Adam Clare (10)
Dishforth Airfield CP School, Thirsk

Poverty, Plague

Poverty is a plague,
There's no way to be vague.
A disease, it spreads through cities and towns,
A deepest sadness is always found.
But this is what sickens me,
Who shall the victim be?
Why the people who once lived there?
Yes, poverty is a snare.
Poverty is a plague,
There's no way to be vague.

Lewis Everett (11)
Doncaster Road Primary School, Barnsley

Monkey Madness

My heart got buried in the sand
When I first saw that monkey's hand
I burst into tears when it got caught
And when the monkey first got bought.

Then I thought, *what would happen next*
And what about all the rest?
The next day I went back,
You could hear everyone clap!
In its eyes there were tears of rain
Plus there was a man with a chain.

The monkey yelped in the cage
While the keeper got his wage
It wailed all day, and all night
I thought to myself, *I just might*
The next day the animal was gone
I took him to where freedom was won!

The monkey had his freedom won
But still he weighed a tonne
As he swung tree to tree
He sprung his knee
And then smiled at me!

Rebecca Mason (11)
Doncaster Road Primary School, Barnsley

All About Litter

L ove to recycle
I need to pick up litter
T ry to help people put their litter in the bin instead of on the floor
T he world will be full of litter if you throw it on the floor
E verything would be clean if you put it in the bin
R ight, let's start!

Laura Murphy (8)
Doncaster Road Primary School, Barnsley

The Tortured Bear

The territory he went through,
Homeless, the pain as sharp as knives.
Endless shows, weaker and weaker he got.
A bit of food means a lot to me.
Relax, I never do that,
Terrified, depressing with the thought of dying in that cage.
Outraged and furious, getting whipped
And not doing anything wrong,
Rejected and heartbroken with no food.
Torture and pain that man gives me.
Ridiculous how he treats me like a punch bag.
Entertainment is painful for me.
Dark times every day.
Beastly is the man who hits me.
Emotionless I don't cry.

Victoria Murphy (11)
Doncaster Road Primary School, Barnsley

Recycling Machine

Bang, clang, smash!
Bottles hitting the path but not for long
There's a new truck in town
He sucks up all the litter
Recycling machine, recycling machine
He does his bit and never makes a mess
Recycling machine, recycling machine
Put your rubbish in him
And don't leave it on the floor
Recycling machine, recycling machine
It will make the world a better place
Use him, the recycling machine, recycling machine.

Elliot Foye (9)
Doncaster Road Primary School, Barnsley

Bear Bounty!

I sat and watched the clock go by,
While others started to tie their tie,
Then *suddenly* the door swung open
And there it was, my ticket token.
Its body an object, its eyes a flare,
But there it was, the dancing bear,
But it was an awful thing I saw,
A broken beast on lumbering paws.

He danced a dance until you see,
The giant beast was set free,
His anguished soul trapped forever,
His tainted paws strapped together.
His eyes, his paws, his body, his fur,
All died together to make one blur.
I tried and tried to watch the show,
But my heart told me to turn my back and go.

My body walking towards the door,
My feet dragging along the floor,
The bear's eyes green with fear,
His nails, claws held with a tear.
I didn't know what to do or say,
So I turned my back and crept away.

Then the owner grabbed my hand
And pulled me towards the band,
I held the whip and whipped his hair,
It wasn't right, it wasn't fair.
I tried and tried to run away,
But the bear's eyes told me to stay.
His eyes like glass,
His snout like brass,
His fur a load of tainted mass.

The dancing bear by being white,
Gives up his camouflage at night
And yet without a thought or care,
He meanders here, he meanders there
And gaily threads the ice flows,
Completely unconcerned without foes.
For after dark nobody dare,
To care for the dancing bear.

Abigail Atkinson (11)
Doncaster Road Primary School, Barnsley

What Is Homelessness?

Homelessness is . . .
No colourful books.
No comfy beds.
No nice DVD.
No colouring pens.
No nice games.
No delicious food.
No nice friends.

Lee Hinchliffe (7)
Doncaster Road Primary School, Barnsley

What Is Homelessness?

No cuddly, comfy beds.
No happy brown houses.
No comfy, colourful clothes.
No happy, helpful friends.
No delicious, colourful food.
No colourful, shiny paper.
No nice colourful clips.
No nothing!

Wiktoria Krawczyk (7)
Doncaster Road Primary School, Barnsley

Untitled

What is being homeless?
No more colourful clothes.
No fresh drinks.
No more red or colourful books.
No colouring pencils.
No colourful paper.
No blue pyjamas.
No dinner.
No school.
No sweets.

Milena Da'Browska (7)
Doncaster Road Primary School, Barnsley

What Is Recycling?

White see-through wrappers
Shining glass bottles
Wet green grass
Slimy fruit
Brown cardboard
Beer bottles
Glass bottles.

Dylan Howson (7)
Doncaster Road Primary School, Barnsley

What Is Homeless?

No colourful toys.
No yummy food.
No soft clothes.
No shiny coins.
No delicious drinks.
No snuggly beds.

Bronwen Dooling (7)
Doncaster Road Primary School, Barnsley

Doing Your bit

Picking up litter, don't make a mess,
Don't paint on the walls graffiti,
Don't rob, give some food to the poor,
Don't go knocking on people's doors,
Don't spit gum on people's lawn,
Don't go scratching people's cars,
Don't go bullying outside of your door,
Pick up litter before there's more,
People don't throw eggs on your window.

Bradley Lawrence (9)
Doncaster Road Primary School, Barnsley

Please Recycle

You recycle
White shiny paper
Dark brown boxes
Clear bottles
Colourful skins
Clear glass
Plastic.

Bethany Markham (7)
Doncaster Road Primary School, Barnsley

Please Recycle

Recycling bright white paper
And see-through glass.
Save your colourful fruit peel
For the compost bin at last.
Collect brown cardboard
Do not waste it.
Plastic bottles clatter
In the recycling bin.

Lucy Edwards (7)
Doncaster Road Primary School, Barnsley

Stop War

S top the fights
T rust the world
O pen your eyes
P ray for peace

W hen will it stop?
A sk the boss why!
R ight, let's stop war!

Eve MacDonald (7)
Doncaster Road Primary School, Barnsley

What Is Homeless?

No comfy snugly beds
No cool white Wii
No playing games
No pink and yellow covers
No blue pools
No noisy phones
No yellow bulbs
No learning schools.

Georgia Blackham (7)
Doncaster Road Primary School, Barnsley

Puppy Dog

Shooting across the room,
his little eyes glistened,
his little eyes glittered,
his paw prints lay on my heart
like footprints in the winter's snow.
His soul lay deep within,
his freedom was with him.

Rachael Lowe (10)
Doncaster Road Primary School, Barnsley

Save The World

S ave the world
A big part, do you want to save the world?
V ery important thing
E verybody take part

T he world is great
H eat that, save the world
E verybody save the world

W orld is a better place
O r do your bit
R emember, save the world
L eave, don't leave things on the floor
D on't do anything wrong!

Phoebe Daly (9)
Doncaster Road Primary School, Barnsley

Please Recycle!

Recycle clean white bottles crashing
Dark brown boxes squashing
White shiny paper tearing
Colourful fruit skins rotting.

Cordelia Faxon (7)
Doncaster Road Primary School, Barnsley

Litter

L itter is harming.
I cecaps are melting.
T iny sea creatures are becoming stuck.
T errible future for planet Earth.
E verything is changing all around the world
R ubbish is travelling in oceans making every living sea
animal in danger.

Amy Kelly (10)
Hade Edge J&I School, Huddersfield

Animals Dying

A nimals dying
N eeding our help
I n all the lands you will see dead animals
M ammals, fish, amphibians, birds!
A ncient animals, don't forget about them
L egless animals still need help
S oggy animals, ancient animals, they all need help

I n the world animals need help
N eed help, that's what animals need

D ogs, dolphins, cats, rabbits, horses
A ll of them need help
N ear and far away animals need our help
G iraffes need tall trees so stop cutting so many
E njoy your planet, don't destroy it
R emember, you only get one.

Karissa Bradshaw (9)
Hade Edge J&I School, Huddersfield

Recycle Litter

R espect to Earth,
E arth is saved,
C ross the country,
Y ou could help,
C ontinents across the Earth,
L ittle you have to do,
E co logic.

L ots of litter,
I t could do damage,
T he world might die,
T he world is in danger,
E nd of the world,
R espect nature.

Maximilian Andrew Bowden (10)
Hade Edge J&I School, Huddersfield

The Dying Rainforest!

Once the rainforest was a happy place
With trees as tall as the sky,
But now all the people have come
And most of the animals will die!

All the snakes and lemurs
Have been forced to move away,
But if you come and help us,
They will be able to stay!

The orang-utans will be able to swing
Through the trees once more,
So if you stop cutting trees,
You will see what nature is for!

We don't have much time
Before the rainforests are gone,
The animals need to stay
At the place they came from!

Rebecca Truby (10)
Hade Edge J&I School, Huddersfield

Plastic Bag

P ollution getting worse
L itter, which is in your bin
A nimals in dangerous situations
S top litter, put it in the bin
T rash! Things in your bin you don't need
I nfesting, getting out of hand
C ompost bins will help the world

B ags that can kill animals
A nimals accidentally choke on plastic bags
G o and possibly go and save the world.

Shaun Burrows (10)
Hade Edge J&I School, Huddersfield

Pollution

P lease help us to save the world
O h dear, the troubles are coming.
L ots of animals in danger.
L itter is taking over.
U gly future ahead.
T ragic times are coming.
I nvest in our future and recycle.
O pen your heart and secure the world
N ever do this again - save the world!

Sally Heywood (9)
Hade Edge J&I School, Huddersfield

Recycle!

R eckless people
E ndangering the Earth
C are for
Y our planet
C ancel all
L itter or
E nd all life.

Harry Crossland
Hade Edge J&I School, Huddersfield

There's Terror In Their Eyes

Blasting, blazing
Dashing, darting
Alarming anger
Vigorous violence
Treacherous terror
Boom! Bang!
There's terror in their eyes.

Demi Clayton (11)
Hade Edge J&I School, Huddersfield

Save The World!

S tinky litter.
A mazing animals dying.
V acation from the pollution.
E co-kid will help you make a difference.

T ime to recycle.
H armful gases are destroying the Earth.
E ncourage others to recycle.

W ithered crops will make no harvest.
O rganise your rubbish into recyclable things and things that are
not recyclable.

R ealise the error of your ways.
L itter is killing the animals.
D o something now or the end is near.

Lewis Wright-Bedford (11)
Hade Edge J&I School, Huddersfield

Poverty - Haikus

Children on the street
What are the dangers they meet?
When will they next eat?

Children living rough
Those children need to be tough
They don't have enough

So sponsor a child
Make a difference today
You know what to do.

Elena-Rose Bunbury (10)
Hade Edge J&I School, Huddersfield

Pollution

P lastic bags are everywhere
O ur world is dying
L itter is being spread
L itter is killing plants and animals
U se the recycle bin
T rees are getting cut down
I know you can help
O h please save our world
N o, don't litter!

Kara Wright (10)
Hade Edge J&I School, Huddersfield

What Have We Done?

Polar bears and Arctic fox,
The world all in a box,
We have burnt down the trees
And disturbed all the bees.
We have gone too far!
The world had to surrender
And we should have been the defender!

Daniel Gratton (9)
Immaculate Conception Catholic Primary School, Spinkhill

Look After Our World

W e have to make sure our world is very healthy.
O ur world can be a better place for everyone.
R ecycle plastic, paper, cardboard and tins.
L earn how to look after our world.
D on't ever throw litter on the ground.

Autumn Lee (9)
Immaculate Conception Catholic Primary School, Spinkhill

Our World

World, world, world, our world is a treat
So keep it nice and neat.
Recycling is good
So try to do it as you should.
If we keep on cutting down trees
There'll be no hives for the bees.
So look after our world and treat it with respect
And enjoy our world.

Amelia Higham (9)
Immaculate Conception Catholic Primary School, Spinkhill

The World

The world is going down at last
And all I do is think of the past
We need to think of those who are poor
We need to think of the war
Now it's time to open the door to new life
Let's help recycle and not pick plants
Let's plant as much as we can
And recycle every can.

Megan Grace Marshall (9)
Immaculate Conception Catholic Primary School, Spinkhill

Stop The Execution

Stop the world having pollution
And help us come up with a solution
It's not so tough
So help us enough
Then we'll stop the execution!

Rebecca Hogg (9)
Immaculate Conception Catholic Primary School, Spinkhill

The World

The world is suffering because of me,
I use all the electricity.
I'm the child that cuts down trees
And kills the bees.
I realised what I'd been doing,
When a crowd of people were booing.
I helped the farmer water his trees
And stopped killing the bees.
I never left the TV on because it would affect the world.

Chelsea Gallagher (10)
Immaculate Conception Catholic Primary School, Spinkhill

I Want The World To Be Green

I want the world to be green
And stop polluters being so mean.
Recycle our stuff,
It won't be so tough,
Now it's the best world I've ever seen!

Georgie Roy (9)
Immaculate Conception Catholic Primary School, Spinkhill

Make A Difference

We hear about rainforests being cut down.
War, poverty and pollution, it's in the news,
You learn about it in school, from books,
Radio, TV and the Internet,
But we could make a difference,
Instead of battle and war you could be friends.
It doesn't matter about the colour or the size of our bodies,
You could save the world by making a difference.
You can be a hero instead of a zero.

Loren Gavins (10)
Immaculate Conception Catholic Primary School, Spinkhill

Litter On The Ground

L itter
I nspire people to not litter
T ell people to pick up litter
T ell people if they buy sweets or chocolate
to put their rubbish in the bin
E veryone should put their rubbish in the bin
R espect our world!

Elle Taylor (9)
Immaculate Conception Catholic Primary School, Spinkhill

Don't Litter

L itter
I t will never help our world
T urn around and say something
T ell the world litter should stop
E veryone, boys and girls
R ecycle it please.

Abbie Watson (10)
Immaculate Conception Catholic Primary School, Spinkhill

Our World

I am the woman that kills the trees,
Which kills people because the oxygen flees,
I'm also the woman that litters all the time
And people think that's a crime.
It's true my friend I don't regret,
Please don't follow in my footsteps.
If we work together we can make this world a safer place
And that means we won't delete the human race,
We could kill our human trace.

Claudia Nicole Ruddiforth (10)
Immaculate Conception Catholic Primary School, Spinkhill

STW

(Inspired by 'The Sound Collector' by Roger McGough)

A stranger called this morning
Dressed in a Santa suit
Got all the animals into a sack
And decided to abandon them
Even though they were too cute!

The scattering of the meerkat
The grunting of the rhino
The roaring of the tiger
The hissing of the snake
The swimming of the turtle
The trumpet of the elephant
The snuffling of the deer

A child read this today
And decided to change
So now thanks to him
The world will do the same!

Victoria Heeks (10)
Immaculate Conception Catholic Primary School, Spinkhill

Save The World

It's a disaster,
We've got to work faster.
What about the water?
Our lives are getting shorter.
All the pollution is making us die,
So start to use public transport,
Instead of poisoning us all.
Maybe have a colder shower,
Or share a bath,
You're on your way to saving the world,
So you can help me spread the word.

Laura Dunham (10)
Immaculate Conception Catholic Primary School, Spinkhill

Climate Change

C limate.
L ose the car.
I nternet is bad for the environment.
M ake each other recycle.
A nimals are dying.
T ry your best.
E nough of it.

C hange.
H elp the world.
A lways recycle.
N ever waste anything.
G et more people to recycle.
E very little helps.

Alex Dale (10)
Immaculate Conception Catholic Primary School, Spinkhill

White Rhinos Are Dying

W hite rhinos
H ot runners
I mpossible to eat
T op horn killers
E xtinction on the way

R hinos are dying
H ot killers
I n a dying period
N ever catch them
O perate to keep them alive
S ave them.

Marc Mappin (10)
Immaculate Conception Catholic Primary School, Spinkhill

Safer Place

Plastic bags rustle on the ground,
There is litter all around,
There are people dying every day,
I used to play,
But now I pray.
There used to be wildlife all around,
But unfortunately now they're in the ground.
I used to love everybody,
But now there is nobody.
I'm sorry God, I'm sorry,
I loved myself instead of others
And now I have no brothers.

Jemma Jennings (10)
Immaculate Conception Catholic Primary School, Spinkhill

Animals

(Based on 'The Sound Collector' by Roger McGough)

A stranger called this morning,
dressed all in red and blue.
Put every sound into a bag
then carried it away.

The roaring of the tiger,
the swift of the turtles,
the trampling of the rhino
and the owls that fly every day.

'A stranger called this morning.
He didn't leave his name.
Left us only silence.
Life will never be the same!'

Britta Schmidt (9)
Immaculate Conception Catholic Primary School, Spinkhill

Save The Animals

(Inspired by 'The Sound Collector' by Roger McGough)

A Stranger called this morning
Dressed in red and grey
Put every sound in a bag
And carried them away

The swooshing of a turtle
The roaring of a tiger
The little squeaks of meerkats
And the purring of a liger

The twooting of a golden eagle
The song of a whale
The howling of a baby bear
And the slithering of an African snail

A child read this today
And decided to change
And then he went round the world
And told them never to kill animals again!

Meg Welsh (10)
Immaculate Conception Catholic Primary School, Spinkhill

I Am Air

I am the air that makes jelly wobble.
I am the air clean and fresh.
I am the air that whips your face.
I am the air that keeps nature safe.
But now thanks to your pollution
I'm growing thinner and soon
I will die.

Tom Shaw (10)
Immaculate Conception Catholic Primary School, Spinkhill

The Crazy Animals

(Inspired by 'The Sound Collector' by Roger McGough)

A stranger called this morning,
dressed in a Santa suit,
he gathered up all the animals
and decided they were too cute,
he took them home for himself,
to feed them their yummy dinner,
but strangely enough
he thought he was a big winner.
The roaring of the lions, the bouncing of the monkeys,
the purring of the meerkats, the swimming of the turtles,
but the stranger was me!

Harriett Petty (9)
Immaculate Conception Catholic Primary School, Spinkhill

Sound Nicker

(Inspired by 'The Sound Collector' by Roger McGough)

A man called this morning,
Dressed in green and blue,
After he left the animal sounds had flew!
The stomping of a white rhino,
The rattle of a rattlesnake,
The banging of a gorilla,
The snapping of an alligator.
A man called this morning,
But didn't leave his name,
Nicked all the animal sounds,
Life will never be the same!

The man was *me!*

Christian Blakemore (10)
Immaculate Conception Catholic Primary School, Spinkhill

I'm The . . .

I'm the tiger that owns the night.
I'm the tiger that starves day and night.
I'm the tiger that gets hunted down.
I'm the tiger that has no life.
I'm the tiger in the lonely night.

I'm the child that supports the tiger.
I'm the child that one day will save the tiger.
I'm the child that will be watching the tiger at night.
I'm the child.

Kristian Richardson (10)
Immaculate Conception Catholic Primary School, Spinkhill

I Am The Child

I am the child that makes poverty,
that kills children many miles away.
I am the child that doesn't recycle anything,
but no one can put me to shame!
I am the child that pollutes the Earth
and doesn't care about the environment!
I am the child that makes racism come true
and I shall carry on until I die!
Should I stop?

Amy R Godber (10)
Immaculate Conception Catholic Primary School, Spinkhill

The Child That Affects The World!

I am the child that cuts down trees.
I am the child that makes people sneeze.
I am the child that pollutes the Earth.
I am the child that makes the world a better place for everyone.

Olivia Eades (10)
Immaculate Conception Catholic Primary School, Spinkhill

I'm The . . .

I'm the tiger that owns the night,
I'm the tiger that starves day and night,
I'm the tiger that gets hunted down,
I'm the tiger that has no life,
I'm the tiger that's alone in the night,
I'm the tiger.

I'm the child that supports the tiger,
I'm the child that will save the tiger,
I'm the child that's against the tiger hunter,
I'm the child.

Ben Gibbons (10)
Immaculate Conception Catholic Primary School, Spinkhill

I Am The Child

I am the child that cuts all the trees,
The child that is always heard.
I am the child that doesn't recycle,
The one that destroys the world.
I am the child that throws all the litter,
I do it because it's cool,
Then suddenly people come up to me
And say, 'You stupid fool!'
But I am the child that feels I can change,
There still is some little time.

James Hammond (9)
Immaculate Conception Catholic Primary School, Spinkhill

This Is Our World

There is so much in the world to be discovered,
Maybe we won't have time for it all to be uncovered,
If we keep going the way we are,
The Earth won't get us very far,
It's been around for so long,
And now people are realising where we're going wrong.

There are so many animals out there,
Thousands of breeds who all just want (out of life) their share,
We're killing them all one by one,
Until eventually there'll be none,
We need to realise what we'd be leaving,
Or else the animals will stop breathing.

Car fumes and houses' smoke all contribute,
It should all be permanently put on mute,
We all need to work together,
Because the Earth's at the end of its tether.
If we all just stop right now,
Imagine what can be achieved . . . *wow!*

Bethany Smith (11)
Kirkheaton Primary School, Huddersfield

Tree-Hugger

Trees help me live!
Different colours, red, green and brown,
I love trees,
Don't chop them down!

Megan Heywood (11)
Kirkheaton Primary School, Huddersfield

Solution For Pollution

The air is filled with dangerous gases,
Every day people let out smoke and ashes,
Letting the world fall to ruins and die,
Listen to the Earth and the people cry.
Planet Earth is suffering from pollution,
We haven't suffered all the consequences,
We need a solution.

April Moore (11)
Kirkheaton Primary School, Huddersfield

Homeless Friends

They sit quivering on the dark, cold doorstep,
As the lonely alley gets even gloomier.
Footsteps scurry past as the wealthy head for home.
Stomachs start to groan as their hunger overwhelms them.
Rats and alley cats start fighting for the scraps,
Smelling the scent of freshly baked baps.
Please help them now, before it's too late,
They wish they too could eat from a plate.

Anna Rose Harrison (11)
Kirkheaton Primary School, Huddersfield

Rainforests

Rainforests are beautiful places,
You see strange plants and different animal faces.
If only it could last forever,
Unfortunately it doesn't last that long,
Because people are cutting down the amazing trees
And if they don't stop now,
The rainforests will fall apart.

Sophie Meachen (11)
Kirkheaton Primary School, Huddersfield

Dad Said . . .

Dad said we can't go on a plane this year,
So we are going on a train.
Me and my sisters all agree,
That choo choos are a pain.
Dad said we would go this way,
So we wouldn't cause as much pollution.
I asked him, 'What is that?' through all my confusion.
He said it is something caused
By fumes from a plane or a car.
'Anyway, stop complaining,' he said,
'We aren't going far.'
I found out lots on our trip,
About pollution and what it does.
So do your part, don't travel far and do the same as us.

Lily Cameron (10)
Kirkheaton Primary School, Huddersfield

Eco Friendly World

E nvironmentally friendly
C ulture
O ver 100 species are extinct!

F ind a way to save our planet
R ubbish is taking over
I s it too late to save the
E nvironment? Please help
N ow or else all that will be left is
D irt rotting away, don't
L eave our planet in despair, no, do
Y our bit.

Tom Wilcox (7)
Malin Bridge Primary School, Sheffield

Rubbish, Rubbish

R ubbish, rubbish
E verywhere I look
C an we recycle?
Y es we can!
C harge people who are litterbugs,
L ess rubbish
E verywhere, everyone will be glad now.

Alfie Smith (8)
Malin Bridge Primary School, Sheffield

Recycle

R ubbish
E verywhere it's found
C an we recycle?
Y es we can
C hange the environment
L ess rubbish
E nvironment is number 1!

Luke Grandahl (8)
Malin Bridge Primary School, Sheffield

Diseases

D irty diseases
I n the streets
S tealing people's happiness
E ven you and me
A fter a few days you'll be
S kipping away
E nd of the illness, we now have our happiness back!

Lauren Baker (8)
Malin Bridge Primary School, Sheffield

Recycle

R ubbish, rubbish, rubbish
E verywhere it's found
C an we recycle?
Y es we can
C hange the environment
L ess rubbish
E nvironment is number one!

Zach Wells (8)
Malin Bridge Primary School, Sheffield

Recycle

R ecycle to help the environment
E veryone can help
C lean up everywhere
Y es we will
'C ause it is good
L itter will be gone
E njoy it and save your No 1 planet.

Ellie Torr (8)
Malin Bridge Primary School, Sheffield

Rubbish

R ubbish
E verywhere it's found
C an we recycle?
Y es we can
C hange the environment
L ess rubbish
E nvironment will die if we don't.

Matthew Godbehere (8)
Malin Bridge Primary School, Sheffield

Recycle

R ubbish, rubbish, rubbish
E verywhere it's found
C an we recycle?
Y es we can!
'C ause it is good
L et's do it now
E veryone can do it now.

Leah Cavell (8)
Malin Bridge Primary School, Sheffield

Recycle

R eally try to recycle, it is to waste.
E veryone has got to recycle.
C an you help the world?
Y ou could help us by recycling.
C ould you help us?
L et everyone join in.
E nvironmentally friendly.

Charlie Beth Taylor (7)
Malin Bridge Primary School, Sheffield

Help The Earth

P ut rubbish in the bin
O pen your heart and recycle
L et the animals survive and recycle
L andfills need your help!
U nderground is terrible waste
T ake care of the world
I mprove the world
O tters are dying without water
N ow everyone will love you for recycling!

Morgan Kniveton (8)
Malin Bridge Primary School, Sheffield

Recycle, Rubbish And Waste

R ubbish is going to the dump fast
E veryone recycle
C an't you see the pollution
Y ou could help!
C an you go and recycle your plastic, paper, tin?
L ook and see what you could do
E co-friendly.

Emily Rose Douglas (7)
Malin Bridge Primary School, Sheffield

Wildlife

W e are trying to help animals but they keep dying!
I am mad with you!
L et the animals be safe from danger!
D on't do nothing, do something!
L ions will roar straight at you!
I will hope you do it!
F riends forever!
E co-friendly!

Lewis James Bellamy (7)
Malin Bridge Primary School, Sheffield

Save The World

R ubbish should go in the bin not on the floor.
E verywhere you look there's rubbish.
C an you save the world?
Y ou should help us by recycling.
C ould you help us?
L ook on the floor and you will see all the rubbish.
E nvironmentally friendly.

Kai Sedgewick (8)
Malin Bridge Primary School, Sheffield

Pollution

P ut rubbish in the bin.
O h please help Earth.
L et us be happy.
L ook, Earth is ruined.
U ndo the mess.
T o make Earth a better place.
I t should be fixed.
O h please make a difference.
N ow do it right and Earth will be happy.

William Armstrong (8)
Malin Bridge Primary School, Sheffield

Recycle, Reuse, Reduce!

R ubbish is everywhere
E arth says come and help!
C an someone do it?
Y ou can help!
C ome right now but don't
L eave rubbish on the ground!
E arth says, 'Thank you all!'

Jodie-Leigh Matthews (8)
Malin Bridge Primary School, Sheffield

Recycle

R ubbish is getting dumped in landfills.
E arth is in danger.
C ycle don't ride in cars, taxis and on motorbikes.
Y ou can make a difference.
C ontrol how much carbon dioxide is in the air.
L ook for eco-friendly things.
E nvironmentally friendly is what you should be!

Joshua Toby Banks (8)
Malin Bridge Primary School, Sheffield

Environment

E arth is dying
N ot one person is helping
V ery serious problems
I am trying, can you?
R ewind and help
O ur environment is suffering
N ot one person on their own can help so work together
M aking landfills is bad
E co-friendly machines are good
N o one is helping
T he environment is dying.

Samuel Taylor (8)
Malin Bridge Primary School, Sheffield

Recycle!

R ubbish is everywhere
E arth needs saving fast
C an you help?
Y ou hopefully can, if so
C ome fast, don't
L eave the Earth in despair
E arth can't help itself.

Tabitha Sophie Hempshall (7)
Malin Bridge Primary School, Sheffield

Environment

R ubbish is everywhere.
E arth is dying.
C reatures are dying.
Y ou could save your planet.
C an you recycle your tin, plastic?
L ove your planet.
E nvironment is dying out.

Lewis Bott (8)
Malin Bridge Primary School, Sheffield

Eco-Friendly

E nvironment
C an you help?
O zone
F riendly people for the environment
R ubbish
I will help
E ven you can help the environment
N ever stop supporting the environment
D on't stop
L ike the environment
Y ou can help.

Danny Parry (7)
Malin Bridge Primary School, Sheffield

Environment

E arth's dying
N ot one person is healthy
V ery serious problems
I am trying to help
R ecycle rubbish like cans and tins
O ur hills are breaking
N ever put on deodorant
M ake the Earth a better place
E nvironmentally friendly
N ever throw rubbish on the floor
T he environment is dying.

Ben Kerrigan (8)
Malin Bridge Primary School, Sheffield

Save The World . . . By Recycling!

Global warming! Global warming!
How can we stop it and what can we do?
We could recycle all our trash,
In the big waste bin that's blue!

We're polluting! We're polluting!
What can we do and how can we stop?
We can stop throwing our rubbish away,
And fill our big blue bins to the top!

But where does it go? But where does it go?
All the things we throw in our blue bin,
They get turned into something new,
And the buyer throws it right back in!

If you recycle your paper and wood,
And the things that come from trees,
Fewer forests will get cut down,
So recycle your trash now - please!

Emily Yardley (9)
Martongate Primary School, Bridlington

Why?

Why buy paper that's been chopped from a tree?
Why buy packaging that's polluting our sea?
Why turn up the heating that melts the ice?
That is global warming and it's not nice!
What is the point in throwing rubbish on the floor?
What is the reason people don't stop and think more?
What can we do to keep the planet going?
Recycle all your things and we'll keep growing!

Becky Dickinson (10)
Martongate Primary School, Bridlington

Recycling

When you've used a piece of paper,
Turn it over and use it later,
Don't just throw it away,
You can use it another day.

Salad, fruit and garden waste,
In the compost bin do place,
Wait about one year or two,
Then put it on your garden do.

Plastic, cans and bits of wood,
Should be recycled and made good,
Giving old clothes and shoes away,
Means they're used another day.

If you don't throw things in the bin,
We can stop this terrible sin,
We can make all this worth,
If you help our Planet Earth.

Amy Louise Stephenson (11)
Martongate Primary School, Bridlington

Saving The World

Sewage, sewage lying in the sea,
A danger to all it could be.

Recycle, recycle to save the world,
How much better it could be?

Litter, litter around the world polluting the sea,
Would it be the end of the world?

Dumping ground, dumping ground,
The world is not a dumping ground.

So recycle.

Sarah Witty (10) & Shauna Keating
Martongate Primary School, Bridlington

But Then They Came . . .

(About an Orang-utan)

That beautiful day we swung
From tree to tree,
As fast as a buzzing bee,
We were as playful as a newborn puppy,
But then they came . . .
And selfishly took our lives away.

I looked around for them,
My beloved ones,
And found their marvellous bodies under trees,
The predators were evil as the ruler of Hell,
I prayed for my life,
Ever since they came,
They ruined my life.

Now I have to look after my life,
The predators, men they're called others say,
Are trying to hurt me,
I want them to go away,
I steal food and put my life on the line,
They ruined and took my lovely life.

Tyler Hallas (11)
Middleton St Mary's CE Primary School, Leeds

Recycling

We had a green bin to put things in,
Recycle your cans,
Recycle your tins,
Put things in your green bin for recycling,
Plastic bottles but not glass,
Cardboard, paper but not grass,
Vegetable peelings not in the bin,
Put them in a compost bin for recycling.

Jack Barry (10)
Middleton St Mary's CE Primary School, Leeds

Will It Ever End?

Left alone in the streets,
Nobody cares,
Nobody speaks,
Up and down the bat beats,
To reveal unwanted pain,
My head sinks down,
No smiles shine ahead,
Will it ever end?

There's no hope for me!
I've woke up in a weird, wacky place,
Food to eat, water to drink,
I can see the light at the end of the tunnel,
Hope is finally there for me,
It's on my side,
Yippee!

There I stand ready to race,
My eyes are heavy,
I'm dizzy, my droopy eyes close,
Will it ever end?

Where's the hope? It's gone again,
My kennel's warm,
There's food and water but I feel so sad,
It's outrageous,
I need a home,
I hope I'll settle in here,
I have somewhere I can call home,
Hooray,
It's finally ended!

Chelsea Boyes (11)
Middleton St Mary's CE Primary School, Leeds

Circus

Everyone goes to see the clown,
They laugh and smile, then they frown,
They see the tiger pacing,
Then their hearts are racing,
At the battered tiger pacing,
Their hearts keep on racing.

Think how a performing tiger is trained,
Beaten, broken and driven insane,
The tigers get furious,
As they would usually roam curious,
Angry, confused and enraged,
Frustrated at existing all caged,
This is not living,
This is just prison.

Nadine Elliott (11)
Middleton St Mary's CE Primary School, Leeds

Racism

Racism is bad,
And it makes people sad,
Everybody's the same,
You can't take the blame,
Children wear glasses,
People have blonde hair,
Schools are for learning,
Not for playing around,
If you're racist,
Your mouth should not make a sound.

Chloe Webster (10)
Middleton St Mary's CE Primary School, Leeds

Homeless

Welcome to the cold, dark city,
You have no windows,
You have no doors,
You have no locks,
All you have is a small, cold box,
You have a bad day at home,
And end up with no bed for the night,
You look through the bins,
Need something to eat,
But only rotting meat,
Your clothes are soggy,
Your clothes are damp,
You look like a tramp,
So who cares if you live?
Who cares if you die?
You're the one cold people forgot,
You're left until you rot.

Kysi Angelica Oldroyd (11)
Middleton St Mary's CE Primary School, Leeds

Recycling

We have a green bin to put things in,
Recycle your cans,
Recycle your tins,
Put things in the green bin for recycling,
Paper, plastic but not glass,
It's good for the environment,
It's good for you.

Katherine Hack (9)
Middleton St Mary's CE Primary School, Leeds

Recycling!

Paper, bottles, plastic and glass,
These are some of the things we learn in class,
Recycling, recycling,
That's the thing!
It's good for the environment,
And everything.

Emma Grime (9)
Middleton St Mary's CE Primary School, Leeds

Horrible War

Ever thought about the real matters,
Around the world all the time,
Where children's hearts are in shatters,
I'm lucky, it's not mine,
When all these wars happen,
It's hard to keep track,
The children's lives blacken,
And start to clutch their back.

Natasha Raistrick (10)
Middleton St Mary's CE Primary School, Leeds

Extinction

Extinction is brown,
It tastes like dead fish,
And smells like pollution,
Extinction looks like dying animals,
And sounds like crows cawing.
Extinction is wrong.

Reanna Howard (8)
Preston Primary School, Preston

Litter

Litter is red,
It tastes like rotten apples,
And smells like a tip,
Litter looks like litter mountains,
And sounds like crackling cans,
Litter is bad!

Olivia Sleight (8)
Preston Primary School, Preston

War

War is red,
It tastes strong,
And smells like smoke,
War looks red and runny,
And sounds like bones dropping,
War is bad.

Callum Hockey (7)
Preston Primary School, Preston

War

War is red,
It tastes like salted chips,
And smells like danger and fear,
War looks like dead soldiers,
And sounds like gunpowder,
War is danger!

Holly Waudby (8)
Preston Primary School, Preston

Recycling

Recycling is black,
It tastes like horrible melted cheese,
And smells like dead rats,
Recycling looks like melted ham,
And sounds like rattling,
Recycling is right.

Eillish Clarkson (7)
Preston Primary School, Preston

War

War is red,
It tastes like dead rats,
And smells like tear,
War looks like the wrong thing
And sounds like an explosion,
War is wrong!

Cale Davidson (8)
Preston Primary School, Preston

War

War is black and white,
It tastes like rotten fish,
And smells like sewage water,
War looks like dead people,
And sounds like guns firing,
War is bad!

Andrew South (8)
Preston Primary School, Preston

War

War is black,
It tastes like blood,
And smells like dead rats,
War looks like dead people,
And sounds like triggers firing,
War is out of order!

Jack Jarvis (8)
Preston Primary School, Preston

Animals And Extinction

Extinction is red,
It tastes like emptiness,
And smells like fear,
Extinction looks like dead animals,
And sounds like silence,
Extinction is wrong!

Isabel Chalmers (8)
Preston Primary School, Preston

War

War is dark black,
It tastes like burning fire guns
And smells of danger coming,
War looks like a bad place
And sounds like shooting bombs,
War is wrong!

Hannah Lyon (7)
Preston Primary School, Preston

Litter

Litter is green,
It tastes like rotten eggs,
And smells like dead rats,
Litter looks like dying animals,
Litter is destroying our view.

Ellie Stevenson (8)
Preston Primary School, Preston

Extinction Of Animals

Extinction of animals is red,
It tastes like oil,
And smells like dead rats,
Extinction of animals looks like dead animals,
And sounds like shooting animals,
Extinction of animals is wrong!

Natalie Cook (8)
Preston Primary School, Preston

Being Homeless

Being homeless is black,
It tastes like black burnt beans,
And smells like old green dust,
Being homeless looks like loneliness,
And sounds like crying babies,
Being homeless is sad!

Lillian Monaghan (8)
Preston Primary School, Preston

Litter

Litter is blue,
It tastes like rubbish,
And smells like sewage,
Litter looks like garbage,
And sounds like crinkling crisp packets.

Litter is killing our animals!

Georgia Coulman (8)
Preston Primary School, Preston

War

War is red,
It tastes like burning bombs,
And smells like firing guns,
War looks like danger coming
And sounds like tanks,
War is wrong!

Olivia Hawksworth (8)
Preston Primary School, Preston

Pollution

Pollution is *black,*
It tastes like fishes' old eyeballs with green beans,
And it smells like oil or petrol,
Pollution looks like poor animals and extinction,
Disease and green rivers or lakes,
It sounds like *bang, crash* and *explosion,*
Pollution is laziness!

Millie Everingham (7)
Preston Primary School, Preston

War

War is red,
It tastes like sour apples,
And smells like gunpowder,
War looks like fire,
And sounds like sirens,
War is wrong!

Kai Bird (8)
Preston Primary School, Preston

Disease

Disease is red,
It tastes like asparagus,
And smells like dead rats,
Disease looks like smoke,
And sounds like people crying,
Disease is pain!

Ellie Broadhead (8)
Preston Primary School, Preston

Litter

Litter is black,
It tastes like a banana skin,
And smells like an overflowing bin,
Litter looks like a mountain of waste,
And sounds like a scrap yard,
Litter is wrong!

Thomas Clifford (8)
Preston Primary School, Preston

Recycling

Recycling is green,
It tastes like mouldy cheese,
And smells like clear air,
Recycling looks like trees,
And sounds like happy lives,
Recycling is good and it saves the world.

Aaron Bradley (8)
Preston Primary School, Preston

Saving The World

How can you save the world? Well:

Recycle, recycle,
It stops rubbish piling up.

Stop war, stop war,
It stops the death.

Don't pollute, don't pollute,
So the animals live.

Help hospitals, help hospitals,
To stop disease.

Give to homeless, give to homeless,
So they're not hungry.

Stop cutting down, stop cutting down,
Trees are home to the animals and oxygen to us.

Don't litter, don't litter,
Or our world will stink.

Save the world, save the world.

Frances Amson (10)
Pudsey Primrose Hill Primary School, Pudsey

Racism

People are getting affected by racism,
So let us stop doing it, and let them have their freedom,
It is not their fault if their skin is a different colour,
They should still be allowed to live freely without treating
them like a monster,
They are just people like us,
So they shouldn't be treated with rudeness,
Let us just *stop!*
And have more smiles and less teardrops,
And no matter where their birthplace is,
Let us not be in disgrace and
Make the world a better place.

Michaella Francisco (11)
St Augustine's Primary School, Leeds

The New Boy

Feeling small, he looked around,
They scowl at him, they shout and frown.

He came from a country far away,
Because of war, he could not stay.

He left his family, his friends, his life,
To escape from trouble, violence and strife.

He thought he would be safer here,
But the truth was yet to appear.

All these names did make him cry,
Racism! Racism! Why oh why?

Jaemien Ezra Serrano (10)
St Augustine's Primary School, Leeds

Racism I Hate!

Racism isn't cool,
Really it is very cruel,
When people don't stick up for you,
You feel like a fool.

Colours of all nations is nice to see,
Languages and people should feel free,
It's 2008, let's get rid of all this hate,
Racism, racism,
I hate, I hate!

Shannon Marie Folan (10)
St Augustine's Primary School, Leeds

Diseases

D iseases developing,
I nsufficient inoculation,
S eeping sadness,
E pidemics encroaching,
A ntibiotic almost absent,
S cabby, scurvy skin,
E ndless emergencies.

Shelby Dyer (11)
St Augustine's Primary School, Leeds

Climate Change

Raining in the summertime,
Blazing in the winter,
The world is becoming rapidly warmer,
People asking why?
All around the world people don't understand,
That the water will consume the land,
If we don't do something soon,
There will be more things like a monsoon.

Michael Hocker (11)
St Augustine's Primary School, Leeds

Recycle

Recycle, recycle,
Let's go for a cycle,
Together we can do something great,
Get rid of pollution - no debate,
So from glass bottles to card,
It's easy not hard,
So whatever the weather,
Let's recycle together,
In this we can save the polar ice caps,
And change the world from all its death traps.

Megan Dowling (11)
St Augustine's Primary School, Leeds

Stuff Matters

I am a girl, I am aged nine, I haven't been round for a long time,
I like most things I see, but there are some things with which
I don't agree.

Racism is one of the things I don't like,
It comes from hatred and fear and causes fights,
Racism's been around for years and years,
It's the lack of knowledge that makes people fear,
Take a step back and try to find out more,
It's amazing what you will learn if you just take time to explore.

Everyone's different, with that I'll agree,
But that just makes everything more interesting to me,
Black, white, Muslin, Catholic, Chinese, Asian, agnostic or Sikh,
We're all just the same when we're walking down the street.

There's enough problems in this world to fight,
So let's put racism to bed tonight,
So if we all stand together, united as one,
I think you'll have much more fun!

Harriet Mae Lobley (9)
St Francis Catholic Primary School, Morley

It's Our World

East and west, north and south,
Listen up, hear me out,
We only have one planet Earth,
It's our world.

Rainforests, being cut down,
Poachers, hunters all around,
Rhinos, leopards, tamarinds,
It's our world.

Carbon footprints, greenhouse gas,
Is this place, meant to last?
Burning fuel and melting ice,
It's our world.

New beliefs, different skin,
Racism, is a sin,
Black or white, pale or tanned,
It's our world.

How to help, what to do?
Need ideas? Here's a few,
Walk, recycle, feed the birds,
It's our world.

Olivia Marchant (9)
St Francis Catholic Primary School, Morley

Our Earth Deserves More

Poverty, hatred, racism, fights,
You know these things are not right.

How can we stop it?
We can show that we care,
The world is very rich,
We can all start to share.

Open your heart,
It's a good way to start,
Skin colour does not matter,
It should not keep us apart,
Why have we been doing this all from the start?
Our Earth deserves more.

Extinction, climate change, destruction, pollution,
You know all these things need a solution.

How can we stop it?
Stop churning out smoke.
Our Earth deserves more than having to choke.
Stop churning up land,
Start planting instead
Before all the animals end up dead.
Our Earth deserves more.

Dominic Philipsz (7)
St Francis Catholic Primary School, Morley

Global Warming - It's Our Responsibility

Global warming is bad for all of us,
A train, a car or a big red bus,
So, remember when you use your car,
You're making our world eat some tar.
There will be summers of snow and rain,
Causing the butterflies pain again and again,
The sky will turn as red as blood,
For in the end, there will be a flood,
Let's all help the scientists find a solution,
To end this human caused pollution.

The last 15 years we have seen many wars,
Mother Earth is unhappy we have spoilt her land,
Look at the world around us today,
To see the anger she continues to show,
We use science against the sky,
Soon it would be hard to live or breathe,
It's time to take a brave stand,
To help our world be there tomorrow,
There will be continuous destruction by water and wind,
Until we shout, 'I need to do my part!'

Elliott Nelson-Addy (10)
St Francis Catholic Primary School, Morley

Our Planet

The world around us looks so fair,
Of our planet, we need to take good care,
We need to find a solution and
A way to get rid of pollution.

We need to recycle rubbish and litter,
To make the air we breathe much better,
We need to find a source of power,
That lets animals live and plants flower.

Isobel Austin (8)
St Paul's Catholic Primary School, Alwoodley

Recycle

Recycle, reuse, reduce and mend,
If you don't want the Earth to end,
Start with your cans, cola or Tango,
In to the recycle bin they can go,
Then they'll melt down and soon will make another can,
An aeroplane or a garden rake,
Next our paper can be recycled too,
Who would know what they can do?
Perhaps make a book or a magazine,
Or a burger wrapper (if it is clean),
What about glass, how might we use this?
Bottles, jars, light bulbs and computer screens - bliss,
Finally we need to reuse plastic,
Especially bags, that would be fantastic,
They can make bottles, tubs and a chair,
At least it would show we are people who care,
Recycle, reuse, reduce and mend,
If you don't want the Earth to end.

Matthew Hallas (9)
St Paul's Catholic Primary School, Alwoodley

Protecting Our Planet

Everything we use should be in the right bin,
Or else we'll find that no one will win,
To save electricity you must switch off that light,
Your bills will be lower,
You know that it's right!
We all need transport and often use a car,
But please only use it if you're going far,
You know it's much better to jump
On your bike, (the air will be cleaner),
Or just take a hike!

Ben Barnes (8)
St Paul's Catholic Primary School, Alwoodley

My Mum's Eco Town

My mum's Eco town will stop making people frown!

Because

We're starting a revolution to stop the pollution!

Why?

We're stopping all the waste to clean up outer space!
We're making it green so all the birds can be seen.

We have got to make it happen,
Now!

Imogen Davenport (9)
St Paul's Catholic Primary School, Alwoodley

Recycle, Recycle

Recycle, recycle, we hear it every day,
Stop throwing some things away they say,
Bottles and paper, plastic all go together in separate bins,
We've got a brown one now for gardening things,
If each of us tried to do our bit,
We would have a happy environment and not any tips.

Bradley Wolstencroft (9)
St Paul's Catholic Primary School, Alwoodley

Trees

T hink if there were no cars, it would be better for the environment,
R emember recycle, it would be better for the environment,
E gg cartons can be recycled, it would be better for the environment,
E vergreens, plants, grow them, it would be better for
the environment,
S ome people take things they don't need, take what you will use,
It'll be better for the environment.

Roisin Brophy (8)
St Paul's Catholic Primary School, Alwoodley

Trees

There once was a tree named Saint Paul,
That stood for years, nice and tall,
But one day the bulldozer came and
It's never quite been the same,
All the trees have been knocked down,
And all the poor kiddies have nowhere to climb,
Since there's no more green to be seen,
It just seems wrong,
See if you can do something about it,
We all know there will never be another tree,
Like Saint Paul ever again,
But there will be other trees, if you help save the environment,
Please we're counting on you.

Elena Holmes (8)
St Paul's Catholic Primary School, Alwoodley

Rainforest - Haiku

Colourful toucans,
Screeching monkeys, rats, bats too,
Save our rainforest.

Elise Greenwood (9)
Scout Road Primary School, Hebden Bridge

Rainforest - Haiku

Colourful and hot,
Noisy, wet, humid and dark,
Save our rainforest.

Alex Hirst (9)
Scout Road Primary School, Hebden Bridge

Rainforest - Haiku

Parrots are screeching,
Many medicines are found,
Save our rainforests!

Lewis Clark (9)
Scout Road Primary School, Hebden Bridge

Rainforest - Haiku

Sticky, dark, hot, wet,
Humid, noisy and grand so,
Save our rainforests!

Oliver Bridge (8)
Scout Road Primary School, Hebden Bridge

Rainforest - Haiku

It's hot at the top
It is dark at the bottom
Save our rainforests!

Jamie Buckley (8)
Scout Road Primary School, Hebden Bridge

A Better World

The Earth will be darker than Hell,
It will be quiet,
Like the dead,
But still standing.

Something terrible
Is descending on the Earth,
Something man-made.

This terrible future,
We must behold,
Can be stopped.

Hold your head high,
Recycle, reuse,
And look after the world we're in!

Don't put cardboard in the bin,
Or an aluminium tin,
You can use it once again!

The world can overcome,
This mass of chewing gum,
Hooray!

Ben Cutler (11)
Southfield Primary School, Armthorpe

Our World!

The world is our life,
Wouldn't you rather live in a lovely open space,
Or a black, dark, lonely hole?
The choice is yours!

The day will fade,
The day will end,
All will be light . . .
But then turn dark.

Recycling your rubbish,
Treasuring the trees,
Keeping the ice,
Preventing pollution.

All these will help,
To save our world,
And make a better future,
For all things we see.

Bang! Crash! Timber!
The trees come falling down,
Acid rain begins to fall,
Like little drops of fire.

In the polar bears' ice caps,
The ice faints into the colossal ocean,
Polar bears begin to lose,
Their poor suffering lives.

Dolphins also dying,
By the stupid, thoughtless people,
Who think it is OK,
To dump rubbish into our oceans.

Cars don't help,
To save our planet,
They wear away,
Our ozone layer.

The sun is getting,
To be too hot,
The sun is growing,
And getting big.

Our world will,
Become destroyed,
All sad and angry,
And dying fast.

In the Third World countries,
No drinking water have they got,
So sadly are they suffering
And having painful deaths.

Are you now seeing a different point?
Has everything become clear?
Will you now think differently,
About the wonderful world?

Katie Wakefield (11)
Southfield Primary School, Armthorpe

Global Warming

The sand plains dead in fear,
Do the right thing to save our world,
Recycle things and let animals live.

Let's walk together to school . . . don't drive,
Each year we are sending about 5,000,000,000 tons of pollution,
Each year we are trying to send a message to people out there,
Listen to us, just listen to us.

People crying because their homes are destroyed with destruction,
Cities devastated with destruction from earthquakes,
Tornadoes and hurricanes.

It's because of us, the people of the world,
We are damaging the environment around us,
People crying because a pool of water is rushing towards them,
The United Nations are trying to send as much help as possible,
But it seems impossible.

Daniel French (11)
Southfield Primary School, Armthorpe

Reducing, Reusing And Recycling

Why don't we reduce, reuse and recycle?
Why do we throw our rubbish on the floor?
The ozone layer is wearing thin,
We don't want a planet war!
By reusing we throw away less,
Reducing means less rubbish,
But recycling is better because we use less resources,
But time will run out for you and me,
All you can recycle . . . here they come;
Paper, tin cans, glass, plastic,
Reusing can be fun,
Come and have a go,
Ice cream tubs, plastic cups,
They all can be reused,
Now let's reduce what's thrown away,
By reusing and recycling we keep reducing,
You may not know it but it's true,
By saving water, sources and other things,
We don't pollute the Earth as much!

Georgie Saynor
Southfield Primary School, Armthorpe

Save The World

Save the world, save the world,
Or it will come to an end.

Crash!
As the ice falls into wide open sea,
As the polar bears have some fun.
The acid rain splinters down on the helpful town
And trees fall in fear, deep, deep down like a diver.

The sparkling, shining sun beams down on a beautiful day.
The world has a blanket of furious fire.

When I played in the park how fun it was but now my fun has ended . . .
Little babies want to play but Mummy says no,
There is glass smashed all over the floor.
Poor little babies can't play.

Pollution is like the dark at night,
So scary, horrible, a terrifying sight.
So recycle all your rubbish.
Littering is a terrible habit to have.

So stop it now
Or the world will come to an end!

Kirby Badger
Southfield Primary School, Armthorpe

Save Our World

Global warming is in the air, all around us everywhere,
You cannot hide from it because it's in your house night and day,
It's in your bed, it will give you a fright,

Global warming can eat you up with no conscience,
You will lie dead as a bat but at least they have their life
Or do they . . .

As the buses go by the cars go past very fast
But do they realise what is happening to our world?
You could share a car to work or walk to school,
Go on buses or trains,
Bye-bye pollution our planet is saved.

Plants are our saviours
Without them we would die,
But racing cars are killing them,
Oh me, oh my.

Recycling is easy, it can be fun,
We just get a bin,
Making sure you can put it in,
You must recycle, that's what you can do . . .
Or else!

Do not litter, it is bitter,
So put it in the bin,
Ban it till you win!

Global warming is a warning, with it we will die,
Diesel is killing us and with it we will die.

So let's work together and save our world!

Eleanor Moorhouse
Southfield Primary School, Armthorpe

The Dolphin

The sea is a lively dolphin
Swift and gentle.
Elegantly gliding along the water
Swishing its beautiful tail,
In the clear moonlight.

Smashing against the rocks,
White foam comes up like acrobats,
Leaping in and out.

Crashing against weak cliff walls,
Sucking up sand and pebbles.
Diving down to the deep,
Shooting back up again into the sky.

Lucy Compton (11)
Walkington Primary School, Walkington

The Sea

The sea is a basking whale,
Giant and blue,
Cutting through rocks.
Silently waiting,
The wind blows,
The whale awakes,
Charging at the mighty cliffs,
Capturing rocks,
Bringing them home
As he breaches the surface.

Anna Williamson (10)
Walkington Primary School, Walkington

The Sea

The sea is a ferocious bear,
Dark and brown,
Bounding towards the shore,
Its power destroying cliffs,
Starting rock falls!

Rising up on its hind legs,
Then toppling over,
Throwing its front legs in the air,
Tossing its colossal weight clumsily,
Striking down cliffs!

The ear-deafening roar,
Shaking the land,
Echoes bouncing off cliffs,
Immense size towering over the mountainside,
Forever living!

Tristan Browning (11)
Walkington Primary School, Walkington

The Sea

The sea is a dark horse
Huge and black
Rearing up, with powerful legs
Galloping across the gloomy shore
Dissolving into pitch-black depths
Too shy to make a sound
Whispering echoes fill the air
Melting away but yet to return.

Delia Richardson (10)
Walkington Primary School, Walkington

Paper?

Where am I?
Thunder in my leaves
Grey skies
I can't breathe,
Towering high in despair
Where are my friends?
Is this a dream?
All alone . . .
Figures with sharp axes
Shouting in angry tones
'Knock it down, knock it down!'
There is nothing I can do
What has happened?
Lying,
Silent,
No leaves, no roots,
What have they done to me?
They have to stop
This is not how I was meant to be
I'm no longer living.

Chloe Bell (9)
Walkington Primary School, Walkington

Turtle Tragedy

My friends are dying
Our hard shells cannot save us
Humans, murderers!

Our safe sea homes are ruined
Act now, before it's too late.

Rebecca Hull (11)
Walkington Primary School, Walkington

Busy, Buzzy Bumblebee

Busy, buzzy, furry, fuzzy,
Businessmen in stripy suits,
Rumbling and tumbling around the jewelled jungle,
Collecting a perfumed feast,
Never stop, or the drop,
Foe or friend, one deadly sting will bring the end.

**Hal Smithson, Joshua Robinson, Daniel Yanes,
Jake Bailey & Edward Douglas (10)**
Walkington Primary School, Walkington

Army Of Ants

Huge army of minuscule troopers,
Marching in sequence,
Slender dark soldiers,
Short matchstick legs carrying them to battle.
Over rough terrain they charge,
Scavenging for prey,
Heavy, huge weights upon their shoulders,
Climbing mountains,
Returning in victory.

Bethany Marris, Anna Williamson & Lydia Stebbing (10)
Walkington Primary School, Walkington

Polar Bears - Cinquain

Cold, white
Stop! Don't kill us,
Forget about the coats,
Please remember our cute faces,
Leave us!

Jessica Bestley (10)
Walkington Primary School, Walkington

Orang-Utan

I am an orphan.
You have taken my mother,
Destroyed my home,
Made my life a misery,
Left me in sorrow,
All alone,
Gradually dying.
Why have you done this to me,
Just an innocent soul?

Giverny D'Auriol (10) & Natalie Webster (11)
Walkington Primary School, Walkington

Litter

Litter, litter everywhere
Bottles, packets everywhere
But nobody cares.

Litter causes damage
Plants, animals will suffer damage
But everyone should care
As our planet dies
Everybody will care.

Victoria Scruton (8)
Walkington Primary School, Walkington

Dolphin Call

As I leap, as I jump,
As I twirl above the waves,
As I dive, as I chase fish,
I am chased by a net.
You heard my call,
Stop killing us!

Sophie Hutchinson (10)
Walkington Primary School, Walkington

The War

Sirens scream,
Guns scream as they crack out.
What in the world has happened
As I hide in my loft?

Flames grow into small infernos
As the bombs are dropped off,
People screaming,
Fires gleaming,
The most terrible sight,
The most horrible fright.

Men die in the hail of bullets,
The deadly cry
Of the dying soldiers,
With crows pecking out their eyes!

I hope one day this conflict will be resolved and gone,
Because there are no winners,
Just losers as they drop a bomb.

Joshua Howlett (9)
Walkington Primary School, Walkington

The Sea Is A Devious Squirrel

The sea is a devious squirrel,
Storing power and nuts,
Bolting at the rocks
As he smashes everything in reach.

The sea is a devious squirrel
As he bounces from rock to rock,
He scuttles smooth and quick.
The sea is a devious squirrel
Sleeping on the shore.

Benjamin Jackson (10)
Walkington Primary School, Walkington

I Think Of . . .

I look out of my window
Cars are passing by,
In other countries where instead they are tanks
And where people die.

I think of all the homeless
That terrorists couldn't care,
And the people in this country,
Think of their despair.

I hate to think of the guns
And the missiles screaming,
Hitting the helpless when they're guilty,
The humans are now bleeding.

I hope to think that one day
That all this will be stopped,
The signals raised,
The gun is dropped
To the floor.

It's all over,
No more war.

Joshua Fairburn (10)
Walkington Primary School, Walkington

The Rainforest

I look to the Earth
I find rainforests, troubled.
They are set alight!
They burn, from wood to ash.
The rainforest collapses,
Like a two tonne truck.
Soil weakens,
Pine burns.

Harry Woolfall (11)
Walkington Primary School, Walkington

Animals And Extinction

The animal kingdom is running low,
From orang-utan to the crow.

The habitats get cut down,
Just to make another town!

The polar bear that lives in the cold,
Snow is melting I am told.

The zebra, hippo and the hen,
Will we see them ever again?

The elegant deer,
Their death is near!

The slithering snake,
More and more we take.

The poachers who I hate,
Let it stop before it's too late!

Edward Prew (10)
Walkington Primary School, Walkington

Racism

Black and white, we're all the same,
Equal people all wanting no pain,
A happy life with no bad words,
We all are delicate as a bird.

We all get hurt with names,
It's got to stop, it's not a game!
People get hurt inside,
It's worse than a cut or stab
As it stays with you forever,
Just on the inside.
We should all be ashamed!

Bethanie Anderson (11)
Walkington Primary School, Walkington

Help Us

The dodos couldn't fly high
So they've waved their wings and said goodbye.

Just think of fish and chips we eat,
But for the cod it's not much of a treat.

Tigers are mostly kitty cats,
But people make them into hats.

All the hippos that like to float,
Are always dreading that gun note.

Just think of dolphins that jump in the air,
But the poachers don't really care.

For kingfishers are bright blue,
But what colour will they be when they're gone too?

So just let the animals live,
It's not just appreciation we give . . .

It's our life.

Zoë Jenkinson (10)
Walkington Primary School, Walkington

Rainforest

I was peacefully sleeping,
In my so called 'home',
I awoke, my baby weeping.
Rattling rang in my ears,
As I drew my eyes downward,
The pain brought tears.
My wiry auburn legs trapped,
The home I had lived in all my life, gone.
I wonder why this orang-utan must die!

Hannah Millington (11)
Walkington Primary School, Walkington

La Vie D'un Caterpillar

Tiny egg protected by Nature's barbed wire,
A tasty treat for the lady with the black spots,
The birth of a many legged waddler,
Bottomless stomach always gorging,
Devouring endless supplies of luscious greenery,
Mother Nature's own lawnmower,
An artistic architect, building delicate homes,
Fantastic winged model,
Showing the world a myriad of shimmering colours.

Lucy Compton, Rebecca Hull, Tomas Gilbert,
Tristan Browning & Conner Beddel-Cook (11)
Walkington Primary School, Walkington

War

War now is on the floor
Tumbling, rumbling, sword fighting and more.
People battling for their lives
Pleading and pleading not to die.

Families crying for them to return
It makes your stomach churn and churn.
Why does he need to leave home?
I wish he was here . . . we feel so alone.

William Adkin (9)
Walkington Primary School, Walkington

War

The sound of guns deafening my ears,
Sadness of a tear stained on my cheek,
My family waiting for me to return,
I long for them to be here beside me
As I sadly drift away,
I wish I hadn't died this cruel way.

Maisie Mae Hobson (11)
Walkington Primary School, Walkington

Think

Think about where we live,
This world full of life,
A beautiful place not that long ago,
Soon it will be a hostile planet,
A blanket of litter all over the world,
Mother Earth is screaming out,
Help me, help!

Next time some rubbish is in your hands,
Think,
Don't litter!

Alex Blake-Barnard (10)
Walkington Primary School, Walkington

The Sea

The sea is a gliding dolphin,
Moving backwards and forwards,
Pulling pebbles in its grasp,
Twirling above the surf,
Jumping over the rocks,
Crashing against the cliff,
Swiftly moving around the sea creatures.

Natalie Webster (11)
Walkington Primary School, Walkington

Litter Is Bitter!

L itter is bitter
I t makes people sad
T hrow it away properly
T hen it's not so bad
E veryone should put litter in the bin
R ecycle it if you can; paper or tin.

Raiyah Butt (9)
Walkington Primary School, Walkington

Turtles

I am a creature who wants to be free
Fill my heart with joy
By letting me roam the sea
I want to live my life in safety
But you're making me worry greatly
The panic, the fear
When the nets are near
I am feeling very miserable
All my days are sad and dismal
Please help me swim free
In the deep blue sea.

Bethany Marris & Anna Williamson (10)
Walkington Primary School, Walkington

What Is Happening?

Azure rivers, glistening in the sun,
Surrounded by willows, skimming my surface,
The soft sandy banks sloping upwards to the valleys,
But now I'm dying,
Polluted by you,
Oil spills clogging up the emerald-green weeds,
You're doing everything wrong,
This is not how I work,
Fish getting caught in plastic bags you throw away after picnics,
Factories dumping, what's that all about?
So? What is happening?
What did I do? Why are you treating me like this?
If you don't act now I will leave you.

Chloë Marchant (9)
Walkington Primary School, Walkington

The Sea

The sea is a mighty whale,
It is dynamic with strength.
Moving elegantly
Slowly and sedately.
A storm breaks, the whale awakes,
Its tail like a rudder.
Colossal jaws opening wide,
Ravenously filtering its prey.
Squirting, spattering, crashing on the rocks,
Breaching the surface.
A fountain of spray,
Like a torrent.

Joshua Robinson (10)
Walkington Primary School, Walkington

Dragonfly

Elegant helicopter glides over the water,
Crystal wings like stained glass windows,
Airborne acrobat,
Hawk of the insect world,
Intricate colours gleam on its shining suit,
Delicate body,
A flying jewellery shop,
Eyes like diamonds,
Wings wide like the ocean,
Hovering over glistening lakes.

Giverny D'Auriol, Tom Gardiner (10), Natalie Webster (11), Lauren Tunnicliffe, Alex Blake-Barnard & Sam Harman
Walkington Primary School, Walkington

Litter, Litter, Litter

Oh dear, what is that I see?
A duck that has been caught in a tree.
Why, oh why, what is the matter?
The duck has been caught by a piece of wire.
I was walking across the bridge,
I saw a very old fridge,
Who could have thrown that in the pond?
Someone of whom I am not very fond.

Litter, litter in the pond,
Litter, litter in the lake,
Why don't people care for goodness sake?
It's such a mess,
It's such a sin,
Why can't everyone use the bin?

Rebecca Bestley (8)
Walkington Primary School, Walkington

Litter

Litter on the streets,
Surrounding my feet,
All caused by you,
What did I do
For you to treat me this way,
Every single day?
And when I go to bed,
Resting my head,
I look at the sun
And wonder what I have done.
All the arguments, fuss and stress,
Wouldn't happen if we cleaned up this mess.

Bethany Marris (10)
Walkington Primary School, Walkington

Our World

Our world is dying,
It's all because of us,
We are stopping birds from flying,
It's time to help, we must!

Polluting the air with greenhouse gases,
Our world is full of war,
But now we're stepping out of the ashes
And realising we can't hold much more.

Factories aren't listening,
To what we are trying to say,
I'd give anything to save our world
And I'd give it any day.

We are choking up our lands,
With red-hot burning fumes,
The future's in our hands,
It could be the worst that looms.

Lauren Tunnicliffe (11)
Walkington Primary School, Walkington

Save The Rainforests!

Rainforests, save the rainforests!
People cut them down
And don't stop to think about others,
Some other people try to save the harmless creatures
That live in that habitat,
It's not fair, they have the same right to be there,
So stop this horrible nonsense
And save the rainforests!

Fiona Anderson (11)
Walkington Primary School, Walkington

Is It Fair?

People in our world who don't have any food,
They're starving and hungry,
Is it fair?

People in our world who eat endless amounts,
They're full up and wasting,
Is it fair?

People in our world are wasting away,
They're starving and hungry,
Is it fair?

People in our world are eating too much,
They're full up and wasting,
Is it fair?

Think how we could help these unfortunate people,
We could make a change to the world,
Is that fair?

Chloë Marchant (9)
Walkington Primary School, Walkington

What's The Difference?

Black and white,
Why do we fight?

No matter your race,
No matter the colour of your face.

Different races fight each day,
Why don't we just be happy and gay?

War between white and black,
Peace and harmony is what we lack.

I don't see how people find it fun,
It feels like being shot by a gun.

Edward Prew & Zoë Jenkinson (10)
Walkington Primary School, Walkington

Open Your Eyes

Some people cry when animals die,
Others just stand and watch.
Although some kill just for a thrill,
Others just stand and watch.
Lots of people chop down the trees
And all the animals can do is flee,
Others just stand and watch.

Some people fish just 'cause they wish,
Others just stand and watch.
Although some protest because they want the best,
Others just stand and watch.
Lots of people do it for food
So their families will be in a good mood,
Others just stand and watch.

So as you can see, open your eyes
And help please!

Kekezza Viant (11)
Walkington Primary School, Walkington

A Butterfly

Developing from cocoon above,
Demolishing to break free!
Magnificent wings waving in the breeze,
A dancer in the summer sky,
Antennae guiding the way.
Studded gem wings posing for the cameras.

Her delicate silk body bursting with tropical colours,
Gently floating in midday air,
Snatching for her prey!
Now full to the brim,
She lies down folding her wings together.

Elena Douglas & Holly Jackson (10) & Grace King (11)
Walkington Primary School, Walkington

Litter, Litter Everywhere

Litter, litter everywhere,
Litter, litter here and there,
Now let's all try and do our best
To make the litter go away.
When you are walking in your street one day,
You might find litter on your way,
Pick it up and throw it away.
When you are in your garden
Don't drop your juice carton,
Put it in the bin,
You can also put in a tin.
Recycle!
Recycle!
Then the rubbish won't go to waste
And the world will be a much better place.

Mia Rose Wallis (8)
Walkington Primary School, Walkington

Save The Rainforest

R ainforest being destroyed
A nimals facing extinction
I n need of help
N o one listening
F orest rapidly depleting
O ur Earth is dying
R uining our environment
E veryone will suffer
S top this destruction
T ime is running out.

Holly Jackson, Jake Bailey & Joshua Robinson (10)
Walkington Primary School, Walkington

Pollution

P ain and death,
O ur world is in excruciating torment,
L ife is important,
L et us help our amazing home,
U nite together,
T o make
I t end,
O therwise
N o one will!

Tristan Browning (10)
Walkington Primary School, Walkington

The Woods

Chopping down the woods is bad,
It makes me feel very sad.
Owls and babies leaving their nest,
Recycling paper would be best.
Now you know how to keep
A place for the animals to go to sleep!

Emma Jenkinson (8)
Walkington Primary School, Walkington

The River

Rivers, rivers they bash and crash against the rocks.
The river widens and widens and widens
And then it crashes down a waterfall
And then it settles to the steady sea.
All the trash and tins and cans cause pollution in the sea.

Daniel Clark (8)
Walkington Primary School, Walkington

Beware Pollution

The sky was always bright and blue,
Nowadays it's up to you.
Pollution in the air is everywhere,
We as a nation should really care.
Let's make sure the rivers are clean,
Do not pollute, it is mean.

Thomas Godber (9)
Walkington Primary School, Walkington

Reduce, Reuse, Recycle!

Recycle plastic,
That's fantastic,
Recycle shoes,
The world won't lose,
Recycle clothes,
Get friends not foes,
Recycle today,
Hip hip hooray!

Katy Hopson (9)
Walkington Primary School, Walkington

Flowers

Flowers, flowers everywhere
Flowers, flowers in your hair
Flowers, flowers next to streams
Flowers, flowers in your dreams
We all like flowers
We all know we do
So go on and grow some too.

Sam Robinson (8)
Walkington Primary School, Walkington

Saving The Planet

We must try to save our planet
We must try our very best
To recycle everything we can
And even Grandpa's vest!

We can recycle all our paper
In the big blue bin
We can recycle other things
Like a silver metal tin.

You can't reuse banana skins
So just throw them in the compost bin
And let the hedgehog sleep tonight
And let them live their life just right!

Natalie Bell (8)
Walkington Primary School, Walkington

Litter

L itter pollutes the world
I t can kill animals
T idy it up
T idy the rubbish on the floor
E veryone is responsible for litter on the floor
R espect the world, pick litter up!

Charlotte Hutchinson (8)
Walkington Primary School, Walkington

Endangered Animals

Save the animals
Help endangered animals
Don't cut down forests
Stop pollution, hunting
And global warming
Play your part today.

Ellie Palmer (8)
Walkington Primary School, Walkington

Water

Melting ice caps are no good
For the polar bears in your neighbourhood.
Unless we start to open our eyes
The sea levels are sure to rise,
So it's really down to you and me
Or we'll soon be living in Walkington by Sea.

Joseph Simms (8)
Walkington Primary School, Walkington

Trouble With Trash

The trouble with trash is, how do we get rid of it?
Bottles and cans all around,
Polluting the Earth and polluting the ground.
Why don't we recycle the old and make something new?
We all can do it, me and you.
Wash out your bottles and cans to make them clean,
So join us so we all can go green.

Joseph Miller (9)
Walkington Primary School, Walkington

Litter Is For Bins

L itter is for bins
I f you don't put litter in your bins it will cause pollution
T he litter is dirty
T he animals can eat the litter and die
E veryone should take their litter home
R ubbish is another word for litter.

Finlay Fotheringham (9)
Walkington Primary School, Walkington

Extinction

Birds peck at peanuts,
Unaware of their future,
Whilst pollution kills.

Parrots fly around,
Just touching the filthy ground,
Watching their homes die.

Nuala Burnett (10)
West Burton CE Primary School, Leyburn

Too Hot - Haiku

I'm sweating. Too warm
Here I am waiting for food
But there is nothing.

Hayley Elizabeth Moore (11)
West Burton CE Primary School, Leyburn

Extraordinary Extinction - Haiku

Tuxedo men go!
Penguins vanished all around
Can you save them, now?

Max Landau (10)
West Burton CE Primary School, Leyburn

Planet Destruction - Haiku

The Earth is dying,
Pollution is killing it!
Now we must stop it!

Adam Dent (9)
West Burton CE Primary School, Leyburn

Litter - Haiku

Muck is on the streets,
Everything very dirty,
Because of people.

Charlotte Pratt (9)
West Burton CE Primary School, Leyburn

Small Predator - Haiku

Big against small, *eek!*
Trying to hide but I can't.
Lots of danger . . . no!

Bethany Jacobs (8)
West Burton CE Primary School, Leyburn

Down The Drain - Haiku

Water vanishing
Because we're using too much
Why don't you just stop?

Millie Beaton (7)
West Burton CE Primary School, Leyburn

Our Dying World

Too much pollution,
Makes the wonderful Earth ill,
So save the planet!

Edward Tiplady (9)
West Burton CE Primary School, Leyburn

The Environment

E is for environment
N is for nature
V is for very bad pollution
I is for I need to look after the environment
R is for reduce, reuse and recycle
O is for other people not caring
N is for not saving the environment
M is for money going towards nature
E is for erasing pollution
N is for not a lot of people caring and
T is for turmoil.

Megan Powell & Bethany Moore (11)
Westways Primary School, Sheffield

Pollution

Pollution, pollution
Put your rubbish in the bin
Pollution, pollution
Recycle paper, card and tin
You can do it, you know you can
If everyone recycles the world will live
So get out your card and tin
And put it in the big recycling bin!

Chloe-Louise Storer (10)
Westways Primary School, Sheffield

The Environment

My cat loves to play
in the garden far away
in the lush green grass of the environment.

The pretty, pretty flowers
spring from the fresh soil
of the environment.

Birds flutter and sing
through the evergreen trees
that survive through all seasons of the environment.

But it gets ruined,
pollution, climate change.
Help to protect the beautiful, lovely environment.

Jacob Pountney (11)
Westways Primary School, Sheffield

Sinking Into Hell

The plastic bags are like scavenging seagulls.
The job of a giraffe torturing the leafy leaves.
Sink into the revolting rotting rubbish like sinking into Hell.
It teases your tremendous taste buds by collecting CO_2.
It wastes waste by collecting tooth tyres with tremendous teeth.
The disgusting death-defying digger taking CO_2 contaminated
rubbish to the dump.
The dump is CO_2's best friend and environment's worst enemy.
Bang! Crash! Smash!
The environment's worst enemy has been released.
Bang! Crash! Wallop!
Hell has been released.
The environment is a ball of grey rubbish.

Kieren Freer (10)
Whitkirk Primary School, Leeds

The Big Crusher

Rubbish, the landfill nightmares!
Diggers sucking revolting, rotting rubbish.
Rubbish crunching underneath tracks.
Plastic bags floating like ghosts.
Can you smell the pong of pollution?
Environment's worst enemy.
CO_2's best friend!

Annie Hawksworth (9)
Whitkirk Primary School, Leeds

The Rubbish Dump

The digger is like a sick giraffe
The sun is a bright yellow round beach ball kicked in the air
The rats are in a race, scavenging for food.

Thomas Whitaker (10)
Whitkirk Primary School, Leeds

Bitter Litter

Litter, litter is so bitter, so I would not care if it was much fitter.
I can see the rubbish ghosts torturing everything.
I can taste the dirt in my throat.
I can feel the JCB scales.
I can hear the scurrying rats scurrying from ghosts.
I can smell plastic rotting away.
Now you know litter, litter is so bitter.

Harmony Musgrave (10)
Whitkirk Primary School, Leeds

Earth's Predator

Garbage-grinder
Seagull-swarmer
Earth-extincter
Air-effecter
Rubbish-riot
It's a landfill site!

Loren Pinder (10)
Whitkirk Primary School, Leeds

Plastic Bags

Food-handler
Recycle-helper
Shop-loader
Light-weighter
Years-user
Litter-picker
Wind-catcher
Environment's friend.

Megan Davies (10)
Whitkirk Primary School, Leeds

The Bin

Landfill-giver
Portable-pusher
Rubbish-cruncher
Wheely-waster
World-destroyer.

Jack Hart (9)
Whitkirk Primary School, Leeds

Landfill Site

Environment destroyer
Animal extincter
Tree tearer
Compost killer
Carbon collector
Mess maker
Rubbish keeper
Smell seeker
Car cruncher
Beetle basher
Seagull attracter
Man-made disaster.

Emily May Dixon (10)
Whitkirk Primary School, Leeds

Litter Mountain

The litter is a metal mountain
I can smell old rotten food
It tastes like unidentified crispy things
I can feel rats scattering under my feet.

Ella Birch (9)
Whitkirk Primary School, Leeds

The Landfill Site

The dirty digger is a powerful rhino
moving across revolting rotting rubbish.
The bags are a layer of rotten, smelly cotton wool
that has once been used.
The JCB moves and crushes the rats.

Charlotte Bagshaw (10)
Whitkirk Primary School, Leeds

Polluted World

I hover in space, full of despair
Haunted by people without a care
Polluted with litter on the floor
Every second there's more and more
A thick grey shadow causing me to choke
Hot in winter, the perishing air gets bitter
Is the world coming to an end
Or how can we make amends?

I scream for help every night
There is no need for us to fight
Every second a child will die
Every day I hear people cry
Is the world coming to an end
Or how can we make amends?

I am the polluted world!

Kimberley Mareya (11)
Whitkirk Primary School, Leeds

The Dinosaurs

Litter . . . the landfill's worst nightmare!
What's happening at the landfill site?
Dinosaurs or seagulls?

Bang! Crash! Smash!
The historic dinosaurs are here
taking the rubbish and dumping it
into the reluctant jaws of the earth.

The dinosaurs are sinking
into the revolting, rotting rubbish.
A wall between Heaven and Hell . . .

Tara Walker (10)
Whitkirk Primary School, Leeds

Prehistoric Landfill

The JCB is a yellow submarine,
sinking in the rubbish, slowly trying to get out!
Rubbish is Joseph wearing the technicolour dream coat,
made out of litter.
The JCB is like a monstrous dinosaur,
trying to catch his prey.
The hopeless rats run free,
spreading germs from rats to the earth.
The wind is dogs throwing their toys
and whistling to get them back!
You can hear the plastic bags
rattling in the cold breeze.

Caitlin Stevens (10)
Whitkirk Primary School, Leeds

Save Our World

When you walk, just stop the talk
and pick up your mess, try your very best.
Our planet is dying, why aren't you crying?
Don't stop trying - to *save our world!*

Don't recycle your bicycle
or recycle your tricycle.
Don't stutter, to stop the mutter.
Our planet is dying, why aren't you crying?
Don't stop trying - to *save our world!*

Don't you care, about the bear
and other animals too, make sure you do.
Our planet is dying, why aren't you crying?
Don't stop trying - to *save our world!*

Eleanor Walton (11)
Whitkirk Primary School, Leeds

Rhinos Are Dying

Rhinos are dying
And I am not lying.
Getting hunted for horns
In the African dawn.
They run fast,
They were born in the past.
But now just think,
That they could be extinct!

Jordan Shaw (11)
Whitkirk Primary School, Leeds

Litter

I float around day and night.
I am cold, it's windy.

I take ages to rot down.
Soon the world will be covered in me.
I am what you throw on the floor.

I wish I got recycled or put in the bin.
I am litter.

Courtney Robinson (10)
Whitkirk Primary School, Leeds

The World's Trash Can

The world is a trash can
made by women and men.
The world is a danger zone
it can rip you to the bone.
You can rake up the rotten leaves
that's how the human breathes.
Don't be lazy, the world is going crazy.
Don't be sad, make yourself glad.
Make a difference by recycling cans.

Tyler Nathan Cording (10)
Whitkirk Primary School, Leeds

Pollution

P eople littering and not caring,
O nly fumes drifting in the air,
L eaves wilting on the trees,
L et's get going to reduce pollution,
U nderstand not to waste energy,
T ell everyone about the problem,
I f you litter you will be fined,
O ur school will do its part,
N ow let's get going to reduce pollution!

Luke Hargreaves (10)
Whitkirk Primary School, Leeds

The Landfill Site

Bottles smashing and crashing like a ball shattering the window,
The smell of pollution around every corner.
The Caterpillar wheels go round like old yo-yos,
The pong of pollution around every corner.
Squawking, scavenging seagulls circle the tip,
The stench of pollution around every corner.
Courageous clashing of machinery pulling its weight around,
Can't you smell the pollution all around?

Nicole Hollick (10)
Whitkirk Primary School, Leeds

Unwanted

I float through rivers, lakes and seas,
Harming wildlife, kicking them out of their homes,
Country after country no one wants me anymore,
People take me away and put me with the rest of the unwanted,
I am pollution.

Ellie Daniels (11)
Whitkirk Primary School, Leeds

Junk Burner

Nose buster,
Taste teaser,
Waste collector,
Muck maker.
Bin lover,
CO_2 creator,
Junk burner,
Seagulls snatcher.
Fridge freezer,
Air attacker,
Gas poisoner.

What am I?
A: dump.

Kristian Fieldhouse (9)
Whitkirk Primary School, Leeds

Littering

L itter is . . .
I n your house,
T here with us,
T here with everyone,
E verywhere,
R otting slugishly,
I nside every landfill site,
N ature feasting on it,
G radually fading away.

Joseph Oldfield (10)
Whitkirk Primary School, Leeds

The Garbage

The bucket squeaks like a rat in a trap,
Shocking shame on a landfill site.

The truck throbs like a headache,
The truck's oil dripping like saliva.

The pile of plastic bags are a high mountain,
Plastic bags floating like white snow.

Environment's worst enemy,
CO_2's best mate.

Rubbish,
Landfill nightmare.

Diggers sucking up revolting, rotting rubbish,
Pong of pollution.

Josh Jordan (9)
Whitkirk Primary School, Leeds

On My Way To School

On my way to school, I fell into a perfect world,
Everyone was nice, including the animals,
Everyone liked me, I liked them too,
No one was fighting, no one was scared,
No one dropped litter, everyone cared,
No pollution in the sky, no litter on the land,
Nothing floating in the sea, no broken bottles in the sand,
My only wish is that my world was just like this.

Daniel Gregory (10)
Whitkirk Primary School, Leeds

Engine Throbbing

Engine throbbing,
Like an unwanted headache.

Shark teeth tyres,
Spitting carrier bags and bottles
Smashing and crashing under sharp shark teeth tyres.
The smell of deadly rubbish rots;
Rots throughout the land . . . landfill site.

Engine throbbing,
Engine throbbing!

Declan Phillips (10)
Whitkirk Primary School, Leeds

Pollution

P ollution is extremely bad
O ne person can change the world
L itter covering the streets
L et's all do our part
U ntidy streams full of plastic bags
T ry to reduce our carbon footprint
I nvolve others to join in
O ur community is helping
N ow you can help.

Sam Brydon (10)
Whitkirk Primary School, Leeds

Young Writers Information

We hope you have enjoyed reading this book - and that you will continue to enjoy it in the coming years.

If you like reading and writing poetry drop us a line, or give us a call, and we'll send you a free information pack.

Alternatively if you would like to order further copies of this book or any of our other titles, then please give us a call or log onto our website at www.youngwriters.co.uk

Young Writers Information
Remus House
Coltsfoot Drive
Peterborough
PE2 9JX

(01733) 890066